DATE NIGHT WITH MOM

by: **Maryann Balbo** & Mason Balbo

illustrated by: Heather Legge-Click

editor: Jerry Campany
graphic design: Tom Patterson

This book belongs to:

- -

In Memory of Ann Piraino - whose beautiful smile inspired us all. May you forever eat popcorn and pickles...while kissing fish.

- M.B.

DATE NIGHT WITH MOM

by: **Maryann Balbo** & **Mason Balbo**
illustrated by: Heather Legge-Click

When Mom picked me up at school, I thought it was just a normal Thursday.

Dinner. Homework. Playing. Bath. Bed.

But not tonight. Mom said she had a surprise. We were going on a "date night."

Now, I didn't know what a "date night" actually was. When Mom and Dad go on a date, my sister and me stay home. We have a babysitter come play with us and order pizza.

Mom said date night was going to be a lot of fun. It was going to be just the two of us doing things together.

Our first adventure was parking Mom's car in the huge parking garage. It felt like we kept driving in circles to the top before we stopped.

We walked by so many cars everywhere and it was quite dark. But, when the elevator doors opened on the street, the sun shone bright.

Mom and I held hands and walked around downtown. There were so many pretty flowers and statues. We saw the courthouse, shops and restaurants.

We wondered what types of jobs people have that work in the tall buildings. I told Mom that when I grow up I want to work in a tall building.

Around the corner was a Farmers' Market. There were fruits, vegetables and plants being sold, but all I could smell was the popcorn. It's mine and Dad's favorite snack. It smelled amazing and tasted even better.

Yummy!

As we kept walking, I could hear music down the street. It was a band with drums, saxophones and guitars. Mom and I stopped to listen to all the instruments.

Mom said she wanted to say hello to a friend who was signing books that he wrote. I got to meet two real-life authors. They were at a book signing at a hardware store that sold toys, candy and stuffed animals.

Mom bought books and some marbles for my sister and me.

I then started getting hungry. Mom said that on date nights people usually have dinner. So, she took me to a store that had an elevator inside.

I said, "Mom, this isn't a restaurant. It's a store!" Mom said, "Just wait. This is the really fun part of our date."

When the elevator doors opened, I couldn't believe my eyes!

There were video games everywhere I looked inside the restaurant. Mom sure knows how to plan a date. I love video games!

We picked a table in the middle that gave me a good view of all the games. I ordered my favorite food-chicken wings. While we waited for our food, Mom let me get our tokens and even play a few games.

I ate all my dinner as fast as I could. It was delicious. Mom said it was date night, so I should order dessert. We shared a peanut butter cake.

My belly was full and I had a cup full of tokens. So, Mom said it was time for competition. We played video games together. I won more than she did and was named the champion! It was so fun.

I was getting tired and had school the next day so it was time to drive home. Mom asked, "What was your favorite part of date night? The chicken wings? All the video games? The music?"
I said, "Those were all nice but, they weren't my favorite."

"My favorite thing about date night with Mom was just being with you. Just me and you Mom!"
She smiled and said, "Mine was being with you."

I wonder what we will do next time on my
DATE NIGHT WITH MOM

Hey Parents!

I hope you enjoyed our story co-authored by my son and I. It was based on an evening with my then seven-year-old son. I found that I just wasn't connecting with him as he was getting older. We weren't arguing and there was no tension, but he seemed to be emotionally distant at times. One day when I picked him up from school I decided that we were going to spend some quality time together. When I announced we were going on a date, he was wide eyed with excitement. I totally winged it, hoping he wouldn't be disappointed with my lack of preparation as we would a big vacation or birthday celebration. Instead, I put down my phone, asked good questions and was emotionally available to him. The change in his behavior during the "date" was so obvious. When we returned home, he was so very excited to share our "date" experience with his father and sister. Then, he did the unimaginable...he wrote a story about our experience. I then knew that we really reconnected during our short 90 minutes of just us.

Mason and I wanted to share our experience to encourage others. Quality time for all our relationships is so very important.

And, I see a "Date Night With Dad" in our near future.

Some Tips...

Spending quality time with your children doesn't have to be expensive or involve a lot of planning. The key is to just enjoy each other's company. Quality time can include going to a park, movies or a walk around the neighborhood.

As a working mother, I have found that just allocating time in my schedule as I would a meeting is a priority I have to make. No fault of our own, but the world spins very quickly. Especially when you are working parent. Days are long and years are short.

Before you know it, our children will be grown and it's more of a challenge to schedule time for just the two of you while competing with friends, ball games and technology. Engaging with them is so very rewarding for all parties but isn't always the easiest to get on the calendar.

When I was researching this book, I found many publications about date night with your spouse but nothing specifically about your child. I wanted to share our experience to encourage others without judgment. Thus, my motivation to share our story.

Some Tips Cont.....

Sharing some of my favorite tips to engage my children.

Asking really good questions to get to know them better and provoke conversation has been my savior in connecting. When they answer, follow up with more questions or even reminiscence about a shared memory.

Feel free to answer the question too! Kids love to hear that their parents are human. Some examples include:

What made you smile today?
What was your favorite vacation we have been on?
What surprised you today?
What was your favorite part of today?
Tell me a weird word you have heard recently?
How did you help someone today?
Did someone help you?
What are you looking forward to tomorrow?
Let's play "answer as fast as you can"?
Favorite color, food, state, shirt, bug, dessert, planet, etc.

Connect With Us

Share a picture of you out on your "Date Night" on Facebook or Instagram...
we might just send you a free gift!

 www.facebook.com/DateNightWithMom

 @MommyBalbo

 www.DateNightWithMom.com

The Authors

Maryann Balbo is a native of Northern New York living in Huntsville, Alabama. She is a mother of two children, Mason and Maxine, and works alongside her husband, Jon, running a local television station. As a busy working professional and mother, she recognizes quality time spent with her children and spouse is invaluable.

Mason Balbo was born in Raleigh, North Carolina and is a current 3rd grader at Holy Spirit Regional School in Huntsville, Alabama. He loves to play the guitar, run with his dog and eat chicken wings.

The Illustrator

Heather Legge-Click is a fine artist with a BA in Studio Art and Art History from The University of Alabama in Huntsville. She focuses mainly on contemporary watercolor studies, large acrylic paintings, and picture book illustrations, but sometimes meanders into the realm of polymer clay and soft sculptures. Her varied works are inspired by her fascination with coexistence, communication, and respect for life.

Made in the USA
Lexington, KY
03 November 2017